ANY CHANGE
FOR THE JUGGLERS

ANY CHANGE
FOR THE JUGGLERS

and Other Poems

SALMON POETRY

For
Síle Ní Dhomhnaill and Éamon Ó Conghaile,
my parents

Published in 1995 by
Salmon Publishing Ltd,
Upper Fairhill, Galway

A catalogue record for this book is available from the British Library.

ISBN 1 897648 31 6

Cover painting by Janet Ross
Photography by Plunkett Smith
Cover design by Poolbeg Group Services Ltd
Set by Poolbeg Group Services Ltd in Palatino 10.5/15
Printed by Colour Books, Baldoyle Industrial Estate, Dublin 13.

ACKNOWLEDGEMENTS

Acknowledgements are due to the following publications in which a number of these poems first appeared:

The Salmon, Stet, Cyphers, Poetry Ireland Review, Writing in the West, Inward Eye, Krino, Ratpit 1, 2, and *3, Force Ten 1, 2, 3,* and *4, New Irish Writing, Space Between U.S.A., Full Moon, Fortnight* and *The Spark.*

Thanks to Jessie Lendennie for her support over the years, John F. Deane for his critical insight and the Killybegs Writers for the support we gave to and took from each other.

Special thanks to Janet Ross for the front cover painting especially commissioned for *Any Change for the Jugglers.* Also to the photographer, Plunkett Smith.

CONTENTS

TODAY

Not ignorant in the sense
                    that we heard
tell of Galileo and Kepler:
we know all the stars are little suns.

Not lonely in the sense
                    that we have
each other sometimes and
the suns and the rains
come to fertilise our bodies.

Not rich in the sense
                    that we believe
to live:
we have no trust in life.

Not afraid in the sense
                    that we play
with laughter bombs
challenge the ghosts in lonely places
and drink till we die.

Not old in the sense
                    that we dress
everyday:
we hide our bodies so as
not to shame a neighbour.

Not loyal in the sense
                    that we crucified
our Christ on Calvary:
we betrayed our inheritance
to impress a ruby or diamond.

Not smart in the sense
                    that we suck
on the system till
it corrodes our bones:
we rot in progression or regression
what's the difference ?
'We are closed for love all day
                    Today'.

MR. ALLIMAR'S LIGHTHOUSE

The night is still ahead.
Sound of sparrows' chirp in
the eaves, gently welcomed him
to a new day.
Alone in a sea-shook house guarded
by a breaking of rock and shoreline:
he wondered when.

His wizened land shook against
the creased bed-spread.
Crooked lines of brown dirt
tried to hide behind his
skeletal windpipe.
In an intense calm he
understood the many languages of the sea.
Seagulls fought over a marrowed mackerel:
no one
fights over him now.

The clock chimed to remind him
the immense isolation he felt
was not total after all.
His mother's portrait fell
from a peeling wall while
dust-mites celebrated
in the sun's rays.

Red-wood beads, dull with age
asked for him another day.
The long lonely sound of a
foghorn, helped him live a whole
life-time in one dusty second.
Morning nurtured noon to a
warm still evening and the dust-
mites had gone away.
Webbed in the trough of time
he was wound around to when
peace would be made.

With scanned images of a timeless clock
and a cracked portrait, there was
no discord in his dying dignity.
On the edge of pain he knew
the hate of evil, the need of company.
Darkness attacked his eyes:
was it too late for snuff and tobacco now?
Crows gathered around his house and
tried to sing at his funeral.

JASMINE

At thirty three thousand feet
the last passenger of the flight,
with take-off still in my eyes,
beneath my hands
your blossom of Jasmine falls
across miles of wind.

A kite that knows the sky
pulls you across mountains
that bear no name
until I name them after you,
houses, where passion knows flesh
that brings the cities down.

My arms
warm from too much handling,
I beg them to grow back to you;
they do not answer.
So I plant your Jasmine in my veins
and wait to watch our garden grow.

SOUL IN THE STREET

Today I catch a glimpse of your soul
in the street
and know it is not at home.
I see it emerge and rend your skin
releasing its mind to wander
as it turns its back on itself.
I hear it speak out of the sun
not in confession or deliverance,
but in heartbeats with a purpose.

I watch you walk across the street
your private voice ringing back the past.
I follow you into your house;
you draw the bath with the skill of a lover-
consulting the bathroom mirror
while you wait.
Then you kneel below me holding
my faith like a river
between your hands.

It is not your Sabbath sun that draws me.
It is the flowers I left in your vase
that do not die.
I watch you take them back
where they came from:
red petals finding their roots
in the wounds of a street without soil.

REGENERATE

If I were a serpent
I would take my tail
Quietly to the undergrowth
Curl it up in a series of circles
One bigger than the other
I would turn the sky on
And watch it screen itself
In Paramount pictures
Giving me what it takes to uncurl
Watch myself grow long
Then juggle the idea
Of eating my tail

WOLF IN THE SKY

I saw a wolf
in the sky yesterday,
he played hide and seek
for a while
then turned into a donkey.
I waited
to see the wolf again,
but a seagull spanned him
with her wings instead.

THE BUTTON THAT SOLD EVERYTHING

Lost seasons between love and hate
Lost hours between day and night
Lost love in a bootless heart
Lost breath to a headless lover

Dried leaves on a trunkless tree
Dried saliva in a closed mouth
Dried skin on a youthful face
Dried eyes in a fatherless child

No smells in the air
No ladybirds in the grass
No wine in the bottle
No smoke in the pipe
No hiding in the dark
No inspiration in the light

Alien residue on an empty street
Alien ashes in an empty grate
Alien clouds in a lost horizon
Alien sounds on a new silence

Hidden vision in stone
Hidden encounters in time
Hidden traps in genius
Hidden prayer in ghosts

No intercourse of moons
No transit of stars
No relief in death
No feeling in life
No stories to be told
No battles to be fought

The candle spits blasphemy
                              On the wall
'My wick was not meant
                    To burn
Like this'.

I LONG TO HOLD SOME POEM

Poems break out
because they have no place else to go.
Like acne,
they get under your skin
then they decide to claim your body.

Wearing your very expensive flesh
they will speak for you,
no one dares disturb them.
Sometimes they will speak out of the ice
and testify against you.
Sometimes they will speak out of the sun
and surrender before you.

Your poems grow up,
they leave you.
You read in the tabloids
how they have become the victims and lovers
you live with.

I say to my poems,
when I meet them in the street,
'I am behind you
you are my hungry mouths
slowly undressing me'.

MY AUNT

My aunt would start to fret
when the first brightness
stretched into the evening.
'Away ye go to the head of the road
and wait till ye see his car.
Don't forget
VIM on top and 375 underneath'.
I'd stand there in the pissing rain
a salty southerly slapping me
in the face
my gym-slip going crazy,
coiling up my waist.
How the hell could I even
see the bloody Volks
never mind
VIM on top and 375 underneath
why wasn't the slime faithful?
I learned a litany of curses
to pile high on his Romeo head.
Soaked to the skin
I'd flop in the door a sodden heap
and utter proudly through my teeth,
'yea, it's definitely him.
He passed by the head of the road
at half past five
on his own; straight from work
VIM on top and 375 underneath'.

Van Gogh Revisited

For ages
you wait in your unweeded garden,
wondering what craze brought you to wife.
You know you can go through with it
because 'better the devil you know'
even better than better; 'the best he is'.

With your butt reading the stars
your petaled rose tattoo inks the sky red –
like a brimming goblet red with wine:
red. Burgundy red-
blood upon a rose, rose upon a bush,
bush bleeding thorns.

Someone moves in the undergrowth.
The burden of their footsteps
causes your heart to pitter patter –
Now you are artist;
Van Gogh revisited.

You take your easel to the undergrowth
with your best Chinese brush
you paint the steps in pitter patter.
Soon your paper is filled with steps
that stop.
Then with a rose between your teeth
you do what you always do.

ONLY STRANGERS TRAVEL

You, the white-robed seminarian,
forge my death certificate
onto blood-ringed paper.

You bury me in the raw wind that cries
down the mountain, throw roses on my coffin,
to make this death smell better.

Your body speaks; your prayers like rhymes
recited in your father's voice,
I do not take them from your lips.

I will argue for my silence
wear my body like a lace shawl.
I am not a stranger to death.

TONIGHT I GET IN TOUCH WITH MY BRAIN

I am smitten
For you in your spirit-shift
Who comes from where the air is sweet

The burden of your absence
Does not heal my discipline
Yet you enter my room a thousand times

How you kneel below my feet
You perform the ceremony
With the fullest motion of your mouth

Willing you my biggest audience
I draw on your lips
With a sudden kind of life

Before we fall from sleep
I dream our mortal souls
Stay up all night

Soon I hear the dawn crack on our whispers
As they settle softly
In the arms of the universe

WHO NEEDS TEETH?
(for Shane MacGowan)

Your name keeps coming up
Out of the gin and tequila
Out of the tabloid ashes
In the cinders
Your name keeps coming up
Down on 'Rain Street'
I saw you in the 'Fall from Grace'
Poster
Cut your profile with a blade
When I came to your mouth
Was careful
Not to cut those vague bits
That genius falling from your lips
No ordinary woozy here
With the abyss opening beyond
You throw back their masks
To the studio owners
Carve your own face-blind
And feast on your fairy tale
Don't cloak us with your silence
Give us the message of your dreams
So we can put them with our own
Your critic mouth fronting
Those crooked teeth
Your jug-ears ringing
The rosary call to the deaf

People say

You are shopping for pearls

'Cause you smashed your mouth in Japan

Out of it in Saki

With the 'Ginger Lady' by your side

With genius like yours – who needs teeth

ANGIE IN THE FOUNTAIN

People say,
she came to grips with her marriage
in the fountain in Eyre Square,
a stone's throw from Prospect Hill,
where she once lived.
They could see it coming –
She couldn't live on cloud 9 forever!

It was far from Greece
and octopus and retsina wine
she was reared
and further still
from belly dancing in Morocco
with glittering diamonds
stuck to her navel.
'She thinks she's the bee's knees,' they say.

Slanted in
the shower of the fountain
neck extended,
jaws dropped open, lion like,
she draws in the jewelled flow
of her world
in every spout of cooling water.
Bewitchdom
in the nature of her gaze.

Later that evening
shivering on a trolley in casualty
half drenched to the skin
and thinking hard on a hot one
in Hogan's
she looked easy on the falling rain.

PITCH BLACK FACES

The sun swallows its light
into its furnace of fire:
little cinders smouldering
across the sky.
The words play hide-and-seek
in the crevice of the page,
and join together in a thick fog.
A cold shiver craps my belly pit
while I pay mind to the pitch
black faces fixed on the trees
that shutter my bedroom window.
Hollows of black, eagle-eyed
and watching from every twig.
They do not budge for ages.
They draw me tight to them,
but I am not afraid:
I know where they're coming from.
Soon I will hear the dawn crack
and paint the trees green again.

MONA LISA IN SOHO

Her suitcase
opens like a lotus
in the Soho Hotel,
her smoke-smelling clothes
perfume her skin of London's smog.
The tap she left dripping
apologises to my touch.

Her doctor tells me
'she's going down the tubes',
but I could tell him we don't intend
going to the underground just yet.

That face is telling me
her back is to the wall;
tonight, then, she's Mona Lisa.
I paint her like a masterpiece
and respect her tears; the energy
in the bones of her face.

Visitors,
distracted, will see her
in the Soho Hotel
step blithely out of her canvas,
smile across the Persian rug and
throw her suitcase with the scrap.

EDUCATING THE LION

It was said by scheming lions
Who set themselves up
As the vortex of knowledge
That the lioness is but
Their spare rib
And bent at that
Lucky for the lion
He had a bent spare rib
To mould the lioness
Into his own image
Anaesthetising her
Forcing the belief
That her epoch is merely
To wed and breed in his captivity
The Lioness is now deriding
The blood and bulging blisters
Of spareribdom
Shedding its psychic scars
Standing in the island
Of her own soul
She now lives with the earth
Counts the trees
And asks the stars for worship

ANGELS OF THE MOUNTAIN

We come to the mountain
in our red hot shifts
singed at the seams.
Hand to wrist, you find me.

We open our mouths
wide as rivers
wet as oceans
driving their salt.

We climb to the sacred place,
you lie hard across dense rock:
altar to skeletal prayers
burning with offerings.

Out of nowhere, a white
butterfly powders your unbound limbs.
How you tease the animal-
under my skin.

Twenty one days
and I know you so well.
Below the lake
we talk.

The trees, how they listen –
From their leaves our whispers hang
like spiders suspended
from their silken draglines.

White powder falls
across my stretched skin:
we choir like angels
below the black lake.

SUZANNA

Suzanna
returns from countless wars,
the last passenger of the day.
Aren't you tired
seeing your beauty leave its scar?

The Southern Cross
is a victim you are sure of.
It did not fall on you,
you claimed it instead.

Listen
where the cricket calls
from its home of bone.
He knows certain creatures
of the air are lying.
For you
he will praise the moon
and let you see the world again.

TALKING FINGER

I find the stars
through the landing window. I wonder
what my driven hands did
before they met you?

I draw on your mouth:
your talking finger paints
Winter across my lips
ablaze with fire.

The moon glides by
dragging at our shadows –
how I feel the cold
between my teeth.

I hum your song for ages:
you do not hear me.
A-freeze. I meet Princess Frost
in the landing window.

WHO MADE SCHOOL?

Your black fringe falls loose
across your forehead.
A creamy bun to ease the pain.
Then the door slams behind you,
rising chalk dust settles your fringe.
You suck a small pebble from your garden
finding little comfort.
One mistake and your knuckles blush
sitting beside a boy is your punishment;
the worst you can get.
How you hate
sitting in that creviced desk
ink-wells dried to a blue black,
like your throat, dehydrated,
in case you touch that monster
beside you.
Then, at break, you stand nose to the window
suck-kissing at your breath.
You are wearing your *bluebell dress*
smelling of America
and you pine for the short-cut home.

CHRIS THE GREEK

I almost forgot,
before I went to sleep,
Chris, the Greek,
with the Italian restaurant.
In tip top shape
he forgets nothing –
never spits
or clears his throat in the morning.
He smokes twenty before 10 a.m.
and eighty before midnight.
'What's the difference
you're gonna die from something: me!
I enjoy myself'.
He never catches cold
only ideas.
'Doctors say
they take ten years off your life',
who cares?
They're the last ten!

Imagining Myself as Lady Godiva

I am Lady Godiva
riding into town on my snow white horse.
I feel I can climb Kilimanjaro,
then jump it.

My white horse shies
when out of nowhere
a faceless phantom stills its hand
and takes me to a place
at the edge of some town,
where people with tongues sharp as blades
scalp me bald as the moon I am after.

What cold I feel here
without my fine hair shift,
where icy cold woods flame in the light
of frosted candles,
freezing spilt tears, white as pearls
across the seedless trees.

I save the locks from my hair
and with my best fine hands
I wave a robe of art, fit for a queen.
I stroke my scalp bristly with growth
rooting in it as it pricks my fingertips.
My snow white horse takes my good news
to places where love rises like mountains.

Rock Music and Sycamores in Boston Common

Early afternoon in Boston Common
sycamores throw our shadows
back at us across oozing bark.

Cauldron of silence simmers:
afraid of the warm feelings
suspended like bats
from the fruited trees.

We sit monk-like
on your warm Indian carpet.
Crusty French bread, pinched white,
waiting to slide across claret-stained tongues.

Rock music rolls
fireworks in our ears –
hemp roller-coasting our heads –
ambushing mosquitoes ride a smoke beam,
clear sucking at our skin.

The sycamores bow a dignity
as my eyes shift through them;
the sun doing its daily suicide
down the sky:
who else will see what I saw?

A Taste of Salt

Tasting the dried salt
on my lips again
nearing the time of leaving.
Readying myself nervously,
knowing well
that choking hardness
rising up my throat:
the feeling now
no longer strange.
Goose pimples raising hairs
on my bared arms
as I dare to risk the separateness.
A feeling of Spiddal,
the smell of the sea
the greenness of clustered ferns
agus torann an chladaigh*
rising up in me.
Taking terminal eyefuls
of Mom and Dad as they
drench me with Knock water,
asking God to give me a safe journey back.
Driving away, blinded,
blinking my eyelids apart:
again, breaking that
contact with my people
and their ways.

*the sound of a pebbly beach.

DEATH'S DOOR
(To the Memory of Éamon Ó Conghaile, my Father)

An old north wind blows tonight
seeking you out,
letting death make great strides
to put the come-hither on you.
Winging you away into
the deepness of space
over the place you have lived always –
beyond the hill –
the frightened apple trees –
across the gazing road field
and the swaying gooseberry bush.
The north wind takes you
past the place where presence was
never stopping.
You paying it a lot of mind
try hard to draw a little back
from the hardness
of this burning grief.
You, in great dread of leaving
draw on a sense of comfort
from those memory driven times.
You'll have no cause to pray now
as church bells ring out
'good-bye' for good.
Someone, someplace, out there in the dark
snatches away the freckles from your face.

No Ordinary Moon

Let's sleep and stay up all night.
Can't we pretend I am the moon
watching lovers trace my path across endless skies
in the hard light of those junkie cities?

Let's have Sushi in a Japanese restaurant,
dance to the end of love in the cherry bowl
keeping our mouths opened.
Let's read Tennyson to our Zen master –
look at your grandmother's ring again.

Let's pretend you are on Zoo television
getting paid for being Ringo Starr.
Let's spread rumours about ourselves
forgetting why we're famous.

Let's act beautiful; fall like grace,
get to Everest, bury your grandmother's ring.
Let's get completely lost
and have no feeling about that.

Let me slip down the sky wild as silk.
I am no ordinary moon
I last longer than the night.

BOSTON
(For Tony Conneely, my brother)

We eat breakfast like a habit
outside at the *Au Bon Pain*.
Our crumbs will never carry
much weight;
the pigeons, making the best of their time,
do justice to them.
Your pancakes slurping in 'Maple Syrup'
make me laugh across streets
where young boys play –
'Back Bay' where my last love poem
stepped out of the harbor.
'Any change for the Jugglers' you say,
three brass coins we give them,
dressed to kill, our love they juggle well,
well as we know,
Boston has been good to us.

SWEET LITTLE SIXTEEN

I felt like Lady Muck
sitting with the fag in hand
on a high stool before closing.
Queen of the throne, I was –
there is my lovely American skirt
and white cheese-cloth blouse –
it took the pain from one fellas eyes
I tell you.
I really felt like Lady Muck Muck
sinking the second rum and black
(just heard the name that day)
holding it high so everyone could see.
God, the thought of having to drink it –
it smelled like nothing on earth.
Glad-eyes trusted themselves on me
wholesale –
tricks peeped down raglan sleeves –
messages from far and near
tickled my ears.
If only I could lip read,
I'd have given them the best sign language
they ever saw.
Suddenly, out of nowhere,
a voice in the mirror said
'Princess. Wait till I get you home,
you just wait' –
I didn't feel like very much, I tell you
looking at the green in the blue in her eyes.

WIDOWED BLACK

The way the wind is blowing
And is warm
Makes me feel good this day
Makes me feel it's time to burn
The cloak of married widowed black
Time to light a roaring fire
Brighter than a spangled sky
And burn to white ashes
The ugly black threadbare cloak
Time to move in flesh
Dance a Palooka across the emperor's head
To a first sense of life felt
In a cloakspan of time
It's time to burn the cloak
Of married widowed black
And blow the white ashes across the earth
Out of the palms of my hands

NO ROCK HUDSON

Hitched a lift from Spiddal to Galway,
halted white butcher's van, low to ground.
Bare-assed beef, wiped clean
dangling on their 'Chiquita' hook.
Gasped breath driver, treble X-rated:
horny handed fingers skim

$\qquad$ my knocking knees.

'I'm going to take you for a spin' –
tilted crooked grin into my leaking eyes.
'Spin', my pulsed tongue uttered,
wishing washing machine in my head.
Thinking street-wise, I said
'let's have a drink first, there's

$\qquad$ great life 'n Salthill.'

Gate-crashed the bus queue, harelike,
Randy come lately on my tail.
'Are ye allright luveen?'
The Bohermore woman said.
'He's trying to abduct me'.

'Don't mind him, the ripe bellied elephant,
he's no bloody Rock Hudson' she hissed,
linking me on the bus
with a well-seeded squeeze,

$\qquad$ before taking me home.

IVORY TOWER

The elements continue to effect me –
The sun. That howling wind
in whose current I am drawn.

A white owl cries the sky
circles me suspect:
funny feeling feast off me.

I have done things before now:
fought off blizzards to reach you –
how I taste you still.

Stars. I had millions of them
lighting in your Ivory Tower
I watched them twinkle and grow big.

Cannot go to you anymore
the sun has burned my eyes –
love hangs from their smouldering sockets.

I feel at home here –
growing light and dizzy
as I do things for myself.

SOME MUD PHONE BOOTH

I often think of travelling penniless
To some mud phone booth
To tell you long distance
How I'm plotting to be your bodyguard
Loving you flesh to flesh all night long
Until exhaustion has left without me

I know why so many people weep
For the love they leave behind
I know why so many people live
In Booze Town or Death Town
This is why I'm here
In this mud phone booth penniless
Thinking about the job
Of being your bodyguard

In answer to my skeletal prayers
The gods will come in floods
And wash me and my phone booth down stream
Winding its way across oceans
To tell you in person that 'I'm here
To be your bodyguard
Loving you flesh to flesh all night long
Until exhaustion has left without me'
And you will say
Holding a fat body of pain inside
'I've been hoping for someone like you'

Auntie's Not In

You did not want to see him –
left me, all of fourteen years,
to hold the kitchen together
while you hid in the down-stairs
bedroom.
'Auntie's not in'
I whinge through the tiny spaces
between my teeth.
'Will I give him a fry', I whisper
through the bedroom door off the kitchen.
Bacon and sausage fat hopping
off my face, splashing *tell him, tell him,*
he bloody knows.
Grease-faced to the eyeballs
I feed the bugger.
I was going to make him more tea
when a *million dollars,*
having popped out the bedroom window,
appeared through the green front door,
clad in a red velvet dress
that traced her waist exactly
swung her thighs lavishly,
right down to the fall-scars
on her proud knees.

The Yin and Yang of a Fish Box

I saw, close up, the look on his face
as he chewed on a chicken wing
at the rock concert in the street.
Dying to slide my hand under
his skimpy t-shirt
to feel every last vertebrae
in his muscular body.
He looked like Leonard Côhen
the way he pulled on the fag.
I dreamt we were in the Chelsea Hotel
biting hard chestnuts and drinking champagne
slip-sliding in pink satin sheets
hymen soaked to budaiascaire
over and over again.
Instead, I take the shakes on a bloody
fish box
and the Chelsea Hotel is only
a flash in the mind.

FLOATING BELOW THE CEILING

Take me back to New Hampshire
with its drinking trees
that spin shadows of yellow and rust
across New England.
Take me back to that room
full of roses and smoke
that do not last the night.
Your hands that stroke the cat
soon to be full of me.
Your silk woven shirt
a thousand sacrifices to the floor.
How your thin face
against a sky wild with stars
follows the swelling moon;
you do not hesitate to love me with it.
Soon, I'm some sort of goddess
from flesh to air I ascend
floating below the ceiling in my soul shift.
In the morning you take away
my perfume on your skin –
It follows you all across New England.

Leaving is the Price

With the energy of a thief
I kneel away the night
in the language of prayer.

But how do I chew on bones
in a saw-dust restaurant
and know they are spare ribs –

slide 'Absolute' down my throat –
compare you to the moon
resting on my shoulder and know

Jesus has not forgotten me –
how do I register a smile and hold it
in some New Year's town –

stop my soul's maladies that speak
across my so distant flesh –
resist the fruits of rough altars and promise

not to die a good looking corpse?
Soon, then, I hear your words on the wind
right after you have screamed;

I call on the moon to stitch them
as they settle softly in my eyes.
What a demanding river they will make!

FRUITS

In Solveign you bring me
champagne and strawberries;
I have become an expert
checking strawberries for possibilities.

Someone is smiling in the corner,
Aztecs waltzing in the kitchen.
I wanted to talk about your hair,
how free the wind has made it.

My fingers bleed strawberries.
I like to hear you say –
when you move about my face,
that not even morning has been broken.

This is our night
the night we found on Live Street,
when you said to me in a kiss
'Love is our address'.

No moon is ever boring, even when we do not hear
the dawn crack on the weight of our distances
so long as we can stick our necks out
for champagne, for strawberries.

Snakes have Time for Me

The half moon hides
putting the sky out
into its hollow of cloud.
A sky, bulging with messages,
takes me to a gallery of pictures,
where snakes polish their brass heads.
Wanton, in their prophet eyes
they stroke their velvety-glazed spots
to curl around my clammy dreams
lapping me up.
I unfold to rattle skin
lower than their bellies
and shine, snake-scaled and heaving,
to search out the half moon –
but she is minding her business
through the black in the sky.

WHO WILL SUCK UP TO ME TONIGHT?

Who will suck up to me tonight
Here in this all-night Japanese restaurant
I wash my hands with a hot flannel cloth
And nothing happens

I only have lunch
I have become expert
In all-night Japanese restaurants
Half the duck is bleeding
The other half is sleeping
"Don't worry darling
The bird didn't feel like very much
Before he met with such sweet company"

I study the cooks for ages
They all have American names
They remind me of some people I know
Who want to be someplace else
Safe in out of the dark
Like me in this all-night Japanese restaurant
Soon I will leave
And face into the rain

I believe in rain
It wets me like grass
When it comes tonight
After I leave this all-night Japanese restaurant
I will like myself dry
Rock like a cradle
Until I finally soothe
And wait to tell some Japanese God
Who when he finally comes
Tells me to settle for the Japanese restaurant
Sucking up to me

MY NEW HAIR STYLE

Beautifully dressed for the occasion
tonight I will live with my new hair style.
I found it in yesterday's kitchen
when you wiped that smirk off your face
and the day wasn't exactly my own.

My old hair style left this morning
after emptying out its drawers,
it walked down the path in the way
of a prosecutor –
I had to say good bye wondering
would it get lonely in the crowd.

Claim me new hair style
I have a story to tell you.
Take me by the hand and lead me
to the museum of fame:
we will dance a Palooka
across the Emperor's head:
absolute heroes our bodies mime.
Afterwards you can take me down
the aisle:
definitely, I'd marry you,
but you know its not my style.

Band on a Chain

Walking down London
living on skid row,
his yellow and white gold
wedding band falls from
a chain link by link
across his lean neck.
His best friend had planted
pansies in his corner garden, free
painted his front door green, free
is umphing his wife, bloody free.
But he knows
what his lousy
pansy-painter-umpher
friend can do
with his stench of pansies and paint –
he can sit tight
on his brass cannonballs
for someday his ass will be
painted green for him
and his hair rooted in pansies, free.

Nursing Waters

Not easy being a lobster
living in this jungle of mad
sea bed where night time
breeds sameness.
My claws, dull as limpets,
guide themselves slowly
across the berthing sea floor
to fiddle away the slackness
of algae, green as Summer.

Its high time I surfaced
and aired my hardened home
stopping you dead in your tracks –
soon, I'll ascend higher than
a mountain; ease myself
out of this pecked torso
to find you frightened
in your white god-like robe
wondering where I have come from.

IN THE NAME OF LOVE

On a cold night in Furbo
catching Winter in my bones,
I put it down to the stars
when the fat cat is about –
how you hear her money talk
after you had promised to die.

Playing Solitaire, I know
it's a long jump from the window
to the mean street:
for death to brag
that she has claimed another
hungry love before it's time.

So put a candle in the window –
let the blind man see
and say a prayer for me –
when my body has gone
my spirit will come back to you
and sympathize.

SNAIL'S SHELL

He came into your life
with an ear-ring and his sailor's eye,
cold as oceans, he's not shy:
he's just a snail's shell
looking for destiny.

Arranging your mornings around him
you give him a course in *creative writing* –
words forever leap and spiral
from you short breath:
words that bear no relation
to that green in his eye.

So you arrange your evenings around him
but, not entirely:
your smile falling like a blessing to the floor
because your breath touches nothing in him –
like an nymphomaniac breaking to confess
you go to the doctor, not to get there.

Fiery eyes that trawl in the dark
wait for the doctor to predict his prophesy:
the doctor being very extravagant, holds your stomach up
and using his best magic,
waits for your writing to disappear.

There is no comfort in this torture
no comfort in being worked over, under white lace
in that room you could never breath in.
Now, you day is your own,
you found it in the *public calendar* where it says
'Your masterpiece is no secret'.

IT'S NOT MY FLESH YOU ARE WEARING

I smell the redness you leave on the wind
when you leave your red-wood tree and visit
where you came from:
that dark earth full of trees and bones
that drink you dry, as lips in Winter.

We met as cheated merchants,
our fortunes found in the streets,
trading things for words full of colour
and poems.
Your feet of a dancer, danced our secret
a thousand sacrifices to the ground.

It's not my flesh you are wearing
when you come up out of the earth and turn
into the sun that does not burn you.
The silence you maintain
will not edit our secrets:
Sue, my name that you do not speak
will leap on you
out of the crumbling red-wood tree.

Good Karma

I hear the poppy fields
eating the night away
while three thousand miles
of hungry love
crosses the static of different oceans.

Tell me, what business are you in
when I fly off the handle
that you turn the other cheek
and fill my mouth with kisses,
is this why they call you 'Doctor of Reason'?